THE LINE MANAGER

A Guide For Successful Employee Management

Sophia Sanchez

Develop For Results International Publishing

This book is dedicated to all those who have a passion for developing others and take action to do so within their organizations, whether they are in a leadership position or not. Current and aspiring business leaders, this book is dedicated to you and to your success!

Introduction

If you are not a line manager, do you need this book?

You may be among the 25 percent who say they are already very good at managing their teams and get the results they want most of the time. Perhaps you are thinking something like the following:

- I already know how to get my team to deliver results while being effective.
- Line managers don't have that many responsibilities, they get a lot of support from top management.
- Why are we discussing employee management? I have work to get done.

You know how to resolve conflicts in your department, and when it comes to managing performance you have no fear. At times, you are asked to help other managers with their challenges. You may even be able to do it all as you sleep. You get great results and have a proven track record. If you already have all the management skills you need, here are a few reasons to keep reading:

- You manage team leads and supervisors and you can't determine why your people aren't as good as you.
- Your team leads always wait for you to make all the decisions and won't address any issues.
- Subordinates can't always relate to, or trust you. Perhaps you've heard you are not fair to the employees and doesn't divide tasks equally. You need to be better at delegating your people and forming better work relationships.
- You are always watching over your team to make sure they are doing their

part because instructions you thought were clear aren't.
- You know your employees could be more engaged and creative but yet, you are doing all the work and they don't show as much enthusiasm as you do.

What's in this handbook?

This handbook provides ideas to help you show up powerfully, and efficiently manage your team. These recommendations are supported by over twenty years' experience with employee relations and management development, and helping people. Included are insights to help you be the best line manager that you can be. Each section is straight forward with actionable tips to help you get started. Instead of philosophical theories, you'll uncover spccific strategies that you can immediately apply with your team in a way that makes people listen and deliver the results you desire. It further discusses the skills which are vital for managerial success, and help supervisors master the qualities which are essential for the management of employees. Different coaching situations faced by managers are discussed along with the variety of approaches which are adopted by supervisors to manage employees.

When it comes to running a successful department, what do you think is most critical?

Any company, no matter how small or big needs people to succeed in this highly competitive era. People make up a company and they are an essential part of it. Employee development therefore becomes a vital part of the process because it contributes to its success. Many managers are not introduced to employee coaching and development as a tool for success. They see it as a waste of time due to the fact that they're not aware of the long-term benefits of investing in their employees or simply willing to disregard the facts.

Every manager wants to utilize their workforce and talent pool, to achieve their objectives, and acquire success. The workforce of an organization is their differentiating factor within the sector, which cannot be copied by its competitors. The employees gradually develop to become the strength of the company, earning it prestige and leadership within the industry.

Technology and resources are factors which can be easily adopted by other organizations, but a trained and developed workforce serves as the most important asset for a company, helping it aspire to and reach new heights of success.

A company might have a skilled workforce, but the key to their performance lies in the technique of utilizing them to their best potential. Organizations which seek to encourage their staff to perform to their maximum potential opt for constant development practices, designed to improve and hone their abilities and have them achieve company and personal goals with admirable success.

The business environment these days is extremely competitive. While there are few disparities in terms of products and services offerings from different companies, the focus of differentiation has shifted to employee retention instead. Business results cannot be achieved without the support and collaboration of a united workforce that aims to deliver the same. Gone are the days when administering employee discipline used to be linked with remuneration. These days "job satisfaction" has found an integrated meaning pertaining to several aspects of work life balance – salaries are a small part of it.

An unsatisfied employee is least likely to maintain his/her position with the current company irrespective of the salary structure. It is estimated that 1 in every 2 employees is dissatisfied with his/her job and is therefore likely to become a part of the job searching segment within a year.

This handbook aims to emphasize on the importance of career growth and advancement in the eyes of the employees. This, by no means, aims to undermine the importance and influence of salaries on employee decisions. Admittedly, about 47% of employees are known to be dissatisfied with their jobs owing to their salary structures. Inadequate compensation can lead to higher turnover rates. It is important to strike a balance between these two aspects in particular and all aspects of job satisfaction in general to promote healthy employment practices.

Smart managers are quick to recognize these changing trends and can therefore come up with the right strategy. The ultimate goal aims at not only recognizing talent in employees but also nourishing and promoting them for greater business gains.

Employee Development

The key to the success or any upper or line manager lies in the development of employees. In this fast- paced world, it is essential for department managers to stay involved in the learning process. Try different strategies and encourage employees to learn new skills. Many platforms offer these skills for free, self-paced and online. Managers should share their expectations so that the employees know what to achieve. When expectations are not shared, there is a communication gap that will lead to a mixed outcome. To run a successful department, managers and employees need to practice effective communication.

Once the employees know their goals, they'll adopt techniques to provide better results. This directly impacts a company's growth. Investing in people's development is not a waste but it is a profitable investment.

Do not consider constructive feedback to be an option in your management toolbox, but make it an important part of your managerial style. No longer do workforce development lies solely with Human Resources. Nowadays, department managers are expected to take on the responsibility of drafting strategies for their departments on how to get the best results from their employees. You should remember as a manager, that sincere and positive feedback is imperative for the growth of your employees. It helps them improve their performance and work on their shortcomings. Positive feedback helps reinstate the good performance, while sincere advice helps to guide the employees on how to ensure improvement in their work efforts.

Keeping Employees Motivated

Motivating people and keeping them motivated in itself is an ongoing process. Not one motivation technique will work for everyone in your department. The key here is to ask employees directly what motivates them. Of course, you are not expected to design a different motivation plan for each person in your department. However, with the information collected, you will be able to get closer to a motivational strategy or strategies that yield the desired outcome. You would be surprise how asking questions can lead to getting answers. Simply ask.

Comment [MS]: Feels like this sh[e]
Not one

Comment [SS]:

Motivation requires efforts from managers and is a crucial part of any department's success, and ultimately the company. As such, managers need to consider the goals of their department before implementing any strategy. Set goals for each employee and motivate them to achieve it in a specific time period. Employees put more effort when they know that there will be appreciation and rewards waiting for them at the end of any task. Always give something in return. Make it a habit of appreciating your people because at the end of the day they are the ones that will ensure everything runs smoothly. Appreciation make workers feel valued, those that get appreciation are the ones who feel compelled to work with more devotion.

Creating the Perfect Base for Your Department

After you have been placed in charge of a department, the first objective is to set a solid foundation. One that aligns with your organization's culture, and serves as the key to the success of your department in the future. Understanding the organization's culture is important in this initial step, because that will dictate how much liberty and control you will have in orchestrating that foundation. In bureaucratic companies with highly concentrated power and decision-making, such departmental strategy may be handed to you for implementation, instead of you designing it. The designing step, however should be comprised of the following:

The purpose of your department

Understand why your department exists and what upper management expects from it. This will define the direction your strategy should take. Without establishing a goal, the company is operating without a purpose. The staff will be operating like drones clueless to what they are working to achieve. This attitude could also start to effect other areas of the organization. Once this broader purpose is understood, it needs to be relayed to the employees. It will serve as a tool to achieve their short-term goals by. They will therefore be on a mission to achieve the

> **Comment [MS]:** Maybe try "is oper without a purpose

target. These set targets in turn are expected to be altered over time as the department and the company's objectives change. Long-term purpose also needs to be identified. This should follow after the generation of every idea to improve on a given task or project. Without this strategy, any department will lack direction and motivation, and therefore loses its worth in the organization. The employees should know their final target so that they are able to work accordingly to reach towards it. Otherwise, redundancy will start to settle, and the department rendered purposeless.

Very similar to the business SWOT Analysis, every manager need to understand the internal and external factors that can potentially impact their department. This includes the quality of the talent pool, available resources, and market conditions affecting your company and department's efficiency. This process also helps to analyze your working environment and gain valuable knowledge about your department's potential.

Combine Strategies to Development

Strategies are part of a department's growth mechanism. These strategies define targets to the employees so that they can work on them to lift up the department. Strategies are created by managers to bring success to the company. But many companies fail to create strategies that are meant for the development of the people that work for them.

It is essential for the managers and leaders to recognize the potential in their employees so that they can create strategies to harvest it in the most effective way. It is not always about the dollar amount, but sometimes a company needs to train its workforce so that they can serve them in a better way. This can be broadly termed as People's Development.

Adopt a Strategy for Development

Managers should adopt strategies for the development of the employees. Employee development is an investment that will turn out to be fruitful in the future. The employees are the most important part of any company and their growth is essential for a department's success. Sometimes you have to create an approach that is not centered towards personal gain and profit alone.

When the managers trust the employees and give them a greater task, then the employees feel confident. This is an attractive strategy that allows the employees to grow and strive for success. The employees of such a department deliver better results. There are certain steps that lead towards development of both – a department and its employees.

Communicating Expectations

The first step in the employee development process is to tell everyone what is expected of them. This is a critical task that every manager need to feel comfortable with. This is part of the process of giving direction to the employees so that they start to work to reach towards their goals. If a manager is not confident in directing his/her employees, there will be no definite result. The employees will move in random direction and the success will be delayed. The employees should be aware of the expectations of the company leaders.

Motivating Your People

Simply trusting your employees can bring a positive change in their attitude and performance. The people that run a company are its employees and it is very important that these employees are headed in the right direction, wearing the right attitude. The leaders in a firm should focus on creating strategies that link back to the development of its people.

Motivating the workforce is a necessary step towards success. For example, the employees of XYZ company work over-time to achieve their targets but they do not get appreciated by their managers. These employees start to become lazy, leave the workplace without completing their tasks, arrive late, and are not serious about their work. This is all because of the lack of motivation.

You don't always need to offer incentives. Sometimes a simple sentence of appreciation can have a huge impact on the attitude of your employees. Encouraging and motivating your employees leads to their development. The employees start to work seriously and focus on their targets. These employees are eager to learn techniques to improve their performance at work. Simply showing appreciation will have a huge impact on the department's success.

The happiness of employees directly depends on the way they are treated at work by their bosses. People are the building block in any organization. If the people of your department are unhappy, your processes won't flourish. Unhappy employees will bring your structure down because they will lack the motivation that they need.

Harvest the Talent

Every manager should practice to harvest the talent of its people. The more a manager understands and apply this concept, the closer he/she will be to success. Every employee in a company has some hidden traits that can only be exhibited if harvested properly. This is the role of the leaders and managers of a company. These managers need to take the employees in the right direction so that they can use their maximum potential.

Act as One Team

In an organization, small or large, acting as one unit is an essential. When carried out correctly, teamwork is an ultimate component of growth. The entire department, from leaders to the employees should work together as a team to achieve the goals of the company. If the top level management has problems with middle level management, it will be hard to get anything done. Unhealthy and unresolved conflicts among a team, is also ground for preventing it to achieve a single purpose.

Lead Your Department

In this competitive era, the employees and managers need to work together in harmony to achieve the main goal of the company. If the departmental staff does not act as one team then they will face many challenges that will lead to the collapse of the organization. As a manager you should have the ability to motivate and give guidance to the employees so that they produce better results. Managers are responsible to create strategies for the employees to achieve effective results. Leading your department does not necessarily mean that you have to do everything by yourself. Any employee that wants to see the company succeed can act as a leader. The manager's role is to empower them to do so.

A leader therefore, should have certain attributes that make him/her stand out amongst the entire workforce. This can either be yourself or a person appointed as the leader of your department; or it can be anyone that possesses these qualities. Team leading qualities are essential in this case. Some of the attributes that a manager must acquire include:

Excellent Communication

As a team leader, a manager should be a person that has the ability to communicate the message effectively to the workforce. This is the most important attribute that any manager should possess. Effective communication helps an organization move forward. If the employees do not understand the target they have to achieve, they will not be able to achieve it. Such message therefore should be communicated clearly and in simple words to the people in your department. Lack of communication often leads to misunderstandings and lack of productivity. A successful manager is one who is able to deliver the message clearly to the employees. When the employees understand the message or any task, they are able to achieve it easily.

Communication also means that the leader is able to adopt a tone that is suitable for the employees. This is part of the big picture of knowing and understanding one's management style and ultimately adopt a tone that is conducive to that style and your workforce. Smart managers motivate those under their direct supervision to reach their department's goals and ultimately achieve the company's goals. Therefore task delegation is important. It encourages a participative style of leadership, which is beneficial to most workplaces. Managers also have to be mindful of favoritism claims. It's imperative to ensure that everyone is treated fairly and rewarded equally for their accomplishments. In doing so, this helps build a sense of trust and reliability that the leader can easily capitalize on.

Role Model

Mangers are expected be enthusiastic and motivated, with a firm belief in the success of the organizations they work for, in order to motivated their employees to contribute to the same. This is a quality that brings about eagerness to the workplace. A positive attitude that lightens the mood of everyone and helps develop a passion for work. Similarly, a dull and de-motivated manager will easily bring the workplace spirit down. When a manager spreads positivity amongst the staff, the workforce puts in more effort to achieve the desired results.

Rules and Regulations

Whenever in place, following a company's policy is a must for the entire workforce. Managers are responsible to follow these regulations, and ensure that their employees do the same. The failure to do so, often lead to bigger legal impact, chances are if the company is not following their own policies, they won't follow mandated laws either. The smart manager stay abreast of all changes to policies and procedures within the organization and ensure they are followed by everyone. This includes administering disciplinary actions when necessary, and documenting every outcome. Documentation is deemed to be the most important step in administering disciplinary actions. Without documentation it's as if the unwanted behavior, nor the corrective disciplinary action never took place.

Decision Making

A team leader is the decision maker in any organization. He/she designs strategies and targets for the employees and then motivates them to achieve those targets. A good leader will be smart in making decisions for the company and its employees. He/she will use all of his/her knowledge and experience to create strategies that are beneficial for the company. A good team leader also needs to be strong minded. This means that he/she should be able to make decision on his/her own. Even if it means letting an employee go for the good of the company. A leader should be able to weigh all the possibilities and then select the best strategy for the organization.

The main goal of coaching is to foster sustainable learning in the team subordinates. Decision making skills should be encouraged in employees to develop their essential qualities and ensure their professional growth.

By encouraging employees to exercise their decision making qualities, managers can coach them to become responsible workers who have the capacity to perform and manage their assigned duties diligently. It also fosters self confidence in the subordinates, reinforcing their trust in their own abilities, which prompts them to perform to their potential.

Air of Confidence

Great managers exhibit confidence through their body language, tone, questioning skills, and work ethics. This air of confidence helps them to direct their subordinates in the right path. Confidence does not come from experience alone, and neither does knowledge. Managers who lack the experience in their fields can still exhibit the confidence needed to lead their teams. The latter requires a strong sense of commitment and self-worth, but can nonetheless be successful. The success is reflected through flexibility, and information sharing with all employees in the department. Therefore the confident and smart manager becomes the architect of a healthy and productive work environment. This type of environment often force employees to get out of their comfort zone and grow.   While experiencing this growth, they are more likely to be engaged and willing to contribute to the department while assuming responsibility for their actions and decisions.

According to Jack Welsh,

"One of the jobs of a manager is to instill confidence, pump confidence into your people."

And this is only possible if the manager is confident himself. Only a confident leader can inspire confidence in employees motivating them to achieve a great goal. A confused manager, lacking the essential skill of being confident, will fail to be an effective addition to the organization, in spite of his experience and other good qualities and skills. Having confidence in skills and abilities will provide self-assurance and self-reliance, which are the first qualities sought by subordinates in their managers and coaching mentors. Therefore, to ensure that you meet your own supervisory goals and also motivate employees to perform to their potential, it is essential that you develop the skill of confidence for guaranteed success.

Implementing Strategies

Great line managers possess the unique ability to connect with the entire workforce to achieve a single purpose. The manager who can manage their team effectively and also the different layers of management is the one that succeeds. It's the ability of managing your managers, regardless of your level of management within the organization. Doing so requires the careful implementation of strategies that must be carried out to meet the objectives of the different layers of management.

In the ancient age of management, senior managers and directors used to be the only ones responsible for involving all other managers and leaders of the company for the implementation of any strategy. They used to determine the short-term and long-term goals of the company and the targets it needs to achieve. In today's workplace, these organizational strategies are scarce. Managers at all levels are expected to develop strategic initiatives for their departments that corresponds to, or supports the organization as a whole. The strategies generated are usually passed on to the middle management or communicated directly to the employees. By whom, and when the information is communicated depends heavily on how much decision-making power is delegated to lower managers.

With training departments becoming more and more scarce in organizations, and human resources roles not expanding; training is slowly becoming part of the managerial tasks and expectations. Depending on the industry, product and services provided, a great deal of this training is being done on the job. This is also another strategic area that requires ample planning that managers should expect to play a role in.

Knowledge Sharing

People's development is all about upgrading the skills, knowledge, and abilities of the employees. It includes ongoing knowledge sharing. That the employees are in a constant learning mode, and are serving the organization more efficiently. Knowledge sharing further helps employees to stay focused on their tasks. Some level of job rotation can also be implemented by managers regardless if there is a training budget in place. In most empowering organizations and industries that are not highly unionized, job rotation should be fairly easy to implement. It also provides job satisfaction and fills the employees with motivation and enthusiasm to improve their performance. Therefore, the employees not only learn new skill but they also serve the organization in a better way. The efforts often produce a self-driven workforce that is confident and engaged in the organization's success.

The Ideal Development Program

Employee development programs are not common in many organizations, let alone by many managers. In its formal form, it's not likely that managers will be able to implement it themselves without the help of upper management. Nonetheless, in this phenomenon lies the true potential of success of an organization. For managers who do not have a development plan in place by their company, they should at least provide ongoing feedback to those they manage. An annual or semi-annual review should not be the only time, nor the first time an employee get feedback on their performance. This goes back to communicating measurable objectives for the individual employees, directly linked to the departmental and organizational goals. Every employee needs to head in a particular direction with proper skills to achieve a mission or a goal. By setting objectives, the manager is actually giving employees something to work for. When the employees have objectives in front of them, they feel more focused. When employees know that they have to achieve a certain target, they work together to reach it. Goal setting is an important part of the motivational strategy for employee development plans.

Managing Conflicts

Conflict resolution is a very important skill that every manager should develop in itself. Resolving conflicts might seem minor to some organization but its effects can be intense. Managers should make it a habit to handle stressful situations and resolve conflicts on their own. Again, some organizations reserve the conflict resolution process to a Human Resources team. In other organizations, managers are partly involved, and usually collect and report information to those in charge of resolving the given problem. Regardless of the role you play in resolving conflicts within your organization, the key here is to resolve workplace problems as they arise. Especially, those with the potential of leading to greater employee relations issues in the future. When resolving conflicts internally, without the involvement of a third party, or government agencies, a time-frame between 24 to 72 hours should be standard.

Identifying High Potentials

Identifying leaders in the workplace is very essential for the growth of the department. There are certain employees that out-perform others and possess leadership qualities. These employees should be carefully assessed by the management so that they can be groomed to be the leaders of the future. Finding leaders from within the department is encouraging for all employees, as then they will see a way up the ladder and will commit themselves to the same. Employee encouragement and motivation have been discussed at every step of this book. This is because it is the most important area that managers need to cover. A happy employee is a productive employee. Managers should focus on preparing their leaders and motivate them in a positive way so that they can improve their performance.

In this regard, timely, and preferably semi-annual performance feedback should be mandatory in every organization. Performance feedbacks are highly effective in encouraging employees to keep working toward a set goal. You cannot expect your workforce to do better if they do not know how they are performing currently. Performance appraisal also helps employees get a clear picture of their career path and the expectations that the management has from them.

Employees can calculate their performance based on the expectations of the managers and improve the quality of their work. The managers on the other hand can help in creating short and long-term goals for each employee based on their current performance. Also, the employees get a chance to be appreciated and rewarded based on the outcome. Performance appraisals help keep employees focused, valued, and motivated to perform better. They also get to know where they stand in the company.

It's a win-win process, the employees know that their performance is being evaluated, and the managers have a clearer picture of the strengths, weaknesses, and motivating factors related to each member of the team.

Importance of Coaching Skills For Managers

Managers are the mentors and serve as coaches for their subordinates, helping them manage to meet their departmental objectives along with the organizational goals. They serve as guides who instruct and encourage employees, and thus bring out their best abilities for the benefit of the company. In order for the managers to perform their duties in an exemplary manner, it is essential to understand that effective coaching abilities are also required. These abilities can be learned and developed over time. Some organizations are slowly investing in developing those skills in their managers; others expect them to acquire the knowledge as part of their personal development. Whenever possible, it is important that managers develop the required skills and qualities which would help them become effective coaches to their employees, and support them to perform at their best.

CRITICAL SKILLS FOR NEW LINE MANAGERS TO DEVELOP

A manager's skill set is their most important asset in the field. With an entire team of subordinates to manage, organize and coach, supervisors need to develop a skill set which includes all the necessary qualities needed to help them become effective managers and good employee coaches.

While certain qualities are considered to be essential for a good manager, a definite skill set is recognized as a success formula for new line managers who is faced with the challenging task of managing the subordinates and taking an active interest in their developmental coaching.

In order to emerge as role models and effective employee coaches, it is essential that the managers either already possess or put in effort to develop skills for succeeding in their goal. A manger needs to be able to relate and communicate with the employees and subordinates in such a way, that it inspires their trust and confidence. This will ensure an easy and efficient coaching effort, which will be developed into the success of the coaching strategy adopted by the organization.

To succeed, it is vital to have a set of essential skills and modify and polish them constantly, in order to remain updated with the latest techniques and skills needed to become good managers and effective employee development coaches.

Self-Awareness

Every manager needs to be well aware of their goals, ambitions, strengths, weaknesses, limitations and drive in life. Only then is it possible for them to be able to become effective coaches and leaders. Through self- awareness, one can achieve many things, for managers, this knowledge will translate to how they manage their workforce.   Only a self-aware manager can help their subordinates realize their potential and help coach them to become self-aware of their own abilities, ambitions, personal goals, and how best to attain them while trying to help the organization meets its objectives. Self-awareness is the key to success, which often corresponds to personal growth. However, every manager needs to develop this skill.

Cultural Awareness

It is essential for every line manager, new or seasoned to be aware of the organizational culture, as well as any societal norms which are given due importance by their subordinates. For any new manager, it takes time to understand the different cultural norms of the organization. Every company has its own unique culture that employees are accustomed to behave within. In order to make your job easier, it's important to step back, observe, and link your managerial style with the organizational culture. An acute knowledge of the organization's culture will help you as the manager to understand the driving factors of the employee workforce, the kind of results the company values, as well as the ultimate objectives of the organization in the industry and how it seeks to achieves its goals.

Empathy

For a good coach and manager it is an essential quality to be empathetic towards their subordinates and team members. It is only by being empathetic that a manager will be able to perform their duties for the regular coaching and development of their subordinates. As coaching and development is an ongoing process, which fosters the effective communication and rapport building between the employees and the supervisor, an empathetic manager will be a sure success in winning the trust of the team by understanding them better. In coaching, empathy is the essential skill and key to ensure effective employee development.

A quote from Stephen Covey showcases the importance of empathy in managers, for getting out the best from their team.

"When you show deep empathy towards others, their defensive energy goes down, and positive energy replaces it. That's when you can get more creative at solving problems."

This quote sums up perfectly how an empathetic manager can inspire their team to perform at their best, and ensure success in their task of developmental coaching. All it needs is an understanding temperament and a skill to recognize the strengths and weaknesses of their subordinates, so that the managers are able to assist and coach them more effectively, ensuring their development as good employees. If you wish to improve your existing coaching and developmental skills or acquire new ones, then make sure that empathy is a skill that you do not forget. The lack of this essential skill can very well prove the difference between a good manager and a failed one.

Questioning

Along with all the other important skills that a manager needs to develop, one very vital one is the art of questioning. By questioning it means that a manager needs to exercise his authority to ask questions and hold his subordinates accountable for their acts, and ask them to explain any negligence and carelessness in the process of performing their assigned duties.

While it is important for a manager to show empathy and confidence, it is even more significant that they exercise a sense of accountability and necessary managerial authority over their team, or the entire coaching objective might very well be lost. While being an understanding manager, it is also important to make sure that you keep the subordinates accountable for all their work. The results and outcomes of their endeavors while being acknowledged and praised, also need to be accounted for.

If an employee or team of subordinates fail to perform at the required level and don't manage to meet their targets, then as a manager focused on developmental coaching of your team, it is essential that you hold them accountable for their lack of performance. Giving the employees autonomy does not mean that they are free to sabotage an established structure. They will and should be held accountable for their actions and any performance related errors as well.

While coaching employees necessitates that the manager develop a good trusting relationship with everyone and inspire confidence from the team, it does not mean that in doing so the manager should compromise his position.

Another important feature that stems out from the skill of questioning is to ask the right questions from your team. While you question your subordinates to inform them how their actions are actually deflecting them from achieving their desired goal, you can direct them towards their path of success by asking them the right questions.

This can be done through intelligent questions, helping them realize their potential and perform at their level best. It is a part of coaching. The art of asking the right questions to coach your team is a must for every new manager and who wants to become a good coach for his subordinates.

While questioning subordinates, it's important to:

- Ask open ended questions: It is important to learn the art of asking the questions which would prove helpful in effective coaching. Instead of asking questions which only encourage yes and no answers, it is important that managers learn the skill of asking open ended questions, which prompt detailed and good answers. Helpful answers from the employees aid managers to learn about the problems faced by them, and ensure effective coaching assistance.

- Ask clarifying questions: a manager needs to ask questions that prompt clarifications and details from the subordinates. These questions prove very helpful in identifying the root cause of the problem, and ensuring efficient coaching support from the manager to his employee team.

- Ask empowering questions: A manager needs to ask questions that help resolve the issues at hand rather than add to the problems. A supervisor can also ask the employee to suggest any solution to the problem and discuss the effectiveness of the action, against any alternative course of action. By discussing the solution with the employee, a manager can resolve all problems without getting into an argument with the team. All it needs is to ask the right question!

- Ask powerful questions: By asking their subordinates powerful questions, managers are able to gauge the reason for the problem and perform their coaching support efficiently, as well as present a strong and supportive managerial position. A manager needs to showcase genuine interest in the responses of his employees and opt for "What" and "How" questions to pose strong queries and get meaningful answers.

By asking the employees the right questions, a manager has a much better chance of getting the desired results. The more refined the art, smoother is the sailing. To become a good manager it is essential to master the art and skill of questioning your employees in such a way that they don't feel threatened, offended or humiliated, but rather see the question as an opportunity to discuss their issues with their manager, and benefit from their supportive coaching assistance. This way, the efforts exerted by a manager are more likely to be effective and foster the success of the manager's attempts to ensure continuous coaching of their team.

According to Chip Bell,

"Effective questioning brings insight, which fuels curiosity, which cultivates wisdom."

By mastering the skill of questioning, every manager can resolve issues and be the role model coach they wish, for their subordinates.

Listening

One of the most critical traits of a good manager aspiring to be an effective coach is their listening skill. Being a manager is not all about dictating your subordinates what they need to do and how they need to do it. Rather it is all about developing a strong employee- manager relationship, which is based on mutual trust, confidence and support. Employees learn to seek guidance from their managers, who see them as their coaches to guide them how to meet with their goals and performance objectives. And all this cannot be possible if the manager is not trained in the skilled art of listening.

Listening is the skill acquired by talented supervisors and managers who recognize that employees need to discuss their work related issues, aspirations, inspirations and motivation and de-motivation factors with an authority, which can lend a sympathetic ear and guide them how to achieve their goals.

When we talk about the listening skills of a manager who is also a coach, it involves the skill of filtering the important and relevant information from the amount of data that they listen to. Listening is important to identify the probable causes of any issues and problems being faced by an individual or the entire team of subordinates. Good managerial skills require interacting with the employees in such a way that they feel valued and are willing to utilize their potential to achieve their own and organizational objectives.

It is only through listening that the manager can gauge an acute understanding of the needs of his subordinate team, and provides them with the kind of support that they need. If a manager is not a good listener, then he cannot possibly be an effective leader. Without having any idea of the different problems being faced by an employee, a manager is in no position to offer any kind of help to aid them in resolving their issues or achieve their goals.

It involves an acute understanding of the employee's stated reasons along with an analysis with the different work dynamics to help the manager make decisions as a good coach. It is only through a thorough knowledge of the employee driving factors, and the issues that they face, that a manager can formulate a strategy which would be effective.

For a manager who wishes to hone their listening skills, it is essential that they master the art. This includes:

- **Sense and understand the words:** A manager needs to pay close attention to the conversation with the employee, and note the actual words, tone, volume, body language and behavior of the employee, so that they are able to make intelligent conclusions about the real cause of the issue.

- **Interpret the conversation:** Listen attentively in order to interpret correctly and draw the right conclusions from the conversation with the employee. Without proper listening, it is not possible for the manager to clearly understand the problems of their subordinates and help them.

- **Respond adequately:** A proper response is only possible if the manager utilizes his listening skill to the maximum while engaged in a discussion with employees. Therefore, listening to the needs expressed are important.

Ralph Nichols, the Listening Legend, has summed up the importance of listening quite succinctly in the following quote:

"The most basic of all human needs is the need to understand and be understood. The best way to understand people is to listen to them."

Carl Rogers has linked effective communication with listening being the most important way to ensure a meaningful and rewarding conversation. He said that:

"Man's inability to communicate is a result of his failure to listen effectively."

He has associated the art of listening with being the essence of a proper and conclusive conversation. This is why managers who wish to be supportive coaches towards their subordinates need to adopt and hone their skill of listening, otherwise they won't have any idea of the intrinsic and extrinsic needs of their subordinates, and would thus be unable to provide the required guidance and support, which is the responsibility of a good coach.

Conversation is the only way that a manager can learn about their subordinates and coach them. The former **CEO of Chrysler Corporation, Lee Iacocca**, has emphasized the importance of listening as a necessary component of effective communication. He said:

"I only wish I could find an institute that teaches people how to listen. Business people need to listen at least as much as they need to talk. Too many fail to realize that real communication goes in both directions."

The Manager as a Coach

Managers face a variety of different situations while looking to perform their duties as effective coaches. Each situation requires managers to act in a specific way and manage their employees to bring out the best in them. The goal of effective coaching is to guide employees how to perform to their potential, and tackle various situations efficiently.

Preventive Coaching

Preventive coaching is a form of coaching, which is applied to address the various employee issues before they reach a critical level. A good manager is more concerned about adopting a preventive approach beforehand, rather than having to correct an issue later, just because adequate corrective action had not been taken at the start.

Managers recognize the importance of identifying the core root of any problem, if they wish to address it effectively. It is vital that in order to manage a problem efficiently, they find out the root causes and devise solutions for them, so that a preventive strategy can help to coach their team.

Preventive coaching focuses on trying to highlight the main cause of the problem, so that preventive action can be taken to reduce the likelihood of the issue from cropping up in the future. As the term itself signifies, preventive coaching is done as a means of reducing the chances of a major organizational concern related to the workforce, from progressing into a problematic stage. Preventive actions could be spread over a matter of weeks or months, in which the manager gets a clear idea of the major de-motivating and stress factors affecting the workplace.

Coaching For Specific Issues

Coaching employees for specific issues involves a great deal of tact on the side of the manager, as they need to identify the needs of their workforce, and determine how best to coach them to meet their objectives. When coaching for this specific task, managers need to exercise all the necessary skills and show all essential qualities of a good manager. Only then is it possible for them to develop a trust relationship with their employees, and hope to get their feedback in order to address the situation at hand.

If an employee or the subordinate team demonstrates a low level of work quality or is experiencing problems in meeting with their targets, a manager will provide the required coaching to help them deal with their problem. The key is to identify the cause of the problem, and help the employee to address it.

The coaching style and technique of a manager depends entirely upon the situation at hand, and how to best manage the issue. Therefore, managers need to be adaptive and flexible coaches, in order to understand the needs of their subordinates better and help them resolve their issues.

Different Approaches to Coaching

Coaching styles and techniques of every manager is different. The most effective coaching approach to be used depends upon the nature of the situation at hand, and the challenging aspects of the issue to be resolved. Managers adopt the most suitable style and approach which help them tackle a situation efficiently, helping them satisfy their subordinates and reach their set targeted goals. Following are some common coaching approaches:

Non-directive

Non-directive coaching is an approach which involves a dynamic change from the traditional directive coaching, which was centered on the control and command style. This relatively popular approach is centered on the concept that autonomy and empowerment are the needs of the day, and that employees need to be given some leverage while performing their tasks.

In non-directive coaching, the manager coaches their team by being open to new ideas and willing to share their experience and skills with the team when they need it. These managers coach through guidance and help the employees make their choices on how best to reach their goals, while performing at their maximum potential. Through non-directive coaching, employees are coached to ensure their sustainable learning, by providing their input in different situations at the time of strategy formulation and decision for a suitable plan of action.

Directive

Directive coaching is the traditional approach which is used by managers and supervisors for effectively reaching targets. Managers, who opt for the directive coaching approach, tend to instruct their subordinates to function according to the specified strategy.

The manager directs the employees on how to perform, and instructs them throughout every step of the way. No input from the employees is encouraged and subordinates are required to work according to the provided instructions of their manager. This method is recommended in situations that warrant disciplinary action, or extreme cases where the manager have to be the decision-maker. At times, with less skilled workers.

Combined

A combined approach to coaching, involves a managerial coaching style which is a mixture of both directive and non-directive coaching. The supervisor adopts the coaching style and approach which best answers the needs of their team, and is identified as an effective coaching style by them, under the circumstances.

The advantages and shortcomings of each coaching style are discussed below:

For managers who choose to adopt a non-directive approach, they will benefit from sustainable learning from employees. This approach fosters autonomous thinking in subordinates, as this style helps them to generate new ideas. Employees will then be prompted to take on initiatives which foster high motivation levels and commitment to departmental goals. This can inspire fierce loyalty, as well as driven and satisfied employees. Long-term, it can mean a staff of highly competent individuals who are capable of assuming multiple roles. While being non-directive, a manager still needs to guide and support their team; otherwise they might fall short of meeting their aspired goals. On the down side, this democratic leader may struggle in difficult times when decisions need to be made quickly. This style is also not suitable when team members have differing opinions on the best way forward.

The directive style (in other words, tell them what to do) is effective in dealing with new workers, with no experience nor understanding of the assigned task. It works well when introducing a new concept or strategy to the employees. In some cases, as a manager, you may have to use this strategy with seasoned employees who are not performing up to par. This style is also a good option for dealing with an underperforming employee when other avenues have been exhausted. The major disadvantages are that employees become dependent on their managers, and therefore not engage in any form of autonomous thinking. If new ideas are valued or necessary for the department, this is of course a terrible style to adopt, as none will be generated. Generally, employees are not encouraged to try out new things, and therefore experience no opportunity for personal growth.

The combined approach on the other hand can offer the best of both worlds, it's a combination of the previous two. Here, the manager is neither telling the employees what to do, nor considering their opinions all the time. Rather, this style is adopted as needed to fit the situation at hand. For instance, a low performer that has moved to the performing zone, should be allowed to have more autonomy in decision-making than they did in the past. The combined approach is ideal and highly transferable across different scenarios. The manager, however, needs to be experienced and skilled to use this style effectively.

T he world is constantly changing and new technologies are being introduced every second. Therefore, line managers need to immerge themselves in learning new skills that they can directly apply to their workplace. As a line manager, you will find that many of the concepts discussed here are not within your immediate control. For many, the company in which you work, will dictate the level of influence you can or will have on your departments. Acquiring and applying the skills presented in this handbook will contribute to one's personal development goal as a line manager. The knowledge is easily transferable from one organization to the next. At DFRI, we advocate a bottom up management style, and therefore strongly encourage line managers and supervisors to work on adopting the set of essential skills and qualities which will make them qualified to provide the critical support to their subordinates.

Managers need to be aware of different coaching situations and provide employees with the required guidance and support needed for improvement in their performance and professional growth.

This means adopting the most suitable coaching approach style which enables them to get the best out of their team. They should always remember to practice the essential skills and habits, necessary for the success of their departments. As a line manager, the expectations are high, your contribution to the bottom line is vital. Your road to becoming great starts with you, when in doubt of how to begin; simply Ask!

About The Author

Sophia Sanchez is the founder of DFRI (Develop For Results International), a boutique advisory firm based in Dallas, TX. DFRI offers on-demand Human Resources and Management services to organizations and individuals. Personally, Sophia has written over 100 articles on performance management, organizational culture, change management, and workplace conflict resolution. She has authored several books, including "The Development Alternative" and has shared her expertize on talent management with many small and large organizations in the U.S. and abroad.

For more information about her work, please visit DFRIHR.Com

To your success,

Sophia Sanchez